NATIONAL GEOGRAPHIC

W9-BPN-945

The Children's Forest

PATHFINDER EDITION

By Peter Winkler

CONTENTS

Kid Power. *This girl was one of the first leaders of the Children's Forest.*

Children in Charge

Kids in Peru have a special reason for taking care of their rain forest. They own it.

By Peter Winkler

Earth has big problems. **Rain forests** are shrinking. Many wild animals are in danger of dying out. **Pollution** spoils air and water. Those are just a few of the problems.

Adults have tried to solve these problems. Their efforts are called **conservation.** That means protecting Earth's wild places, plants, and animals.

Conservation is tough. In fact, it's one of the hardest challenges facing the world today. Protecting nature can require that people change how they live. Doing so can cost time and money.

Despite the difficulties, people have made some progress in taking care of our planet. Some rivers, for example, are now cleaner than before. Yet there's much more work left to do.

So how can humans improve Earth's health? Joaquín Leguía (HWA keen luh GWEE uh) has an idea. He does conservation in South America.

Leguia says kids are the key to saving our planet. He thinks children who love nature will take better care of it—both now and later. So he finds ways to help kids love nature.

The best way to do that, Leguía says, is to give kids a piece of nature. It could be a forest, a field, or even a small garden. The main thing is that kids own it, explore it, and care for it.

Getting Around. *Indian children paddle a canoe made from a tree trunk.*

Rain Forests

Leguía began testing his idea in 2001. He talked with people in the southeastern part of Peru. That's a country in South America.

The people Leguía met live in a rain forest. A rain forest is a wooded area that gets at least four inches of rain a month. Most rain forests are tropical. That means they are in places which are warm all year long.

Rain forests are important in many ways. They make oxygen for us to breathe. And they take harmful gases from our air.

Rain forests are also habitats. Those are places where plants and animals live. Roughly half of Earth's plant and animal species, or kinds, live in rain forests.

Despite all this, humans are destroying rain forests. The amount of rain forest lost each year is roughly the size of Florida.

Leguía asked the people to set aside part of the rain forest for children. At first, adults said no. They needed land for hunting and finding food. But they later gave the kids a large piece of land. It is now called the Children's Forest.

Who's the Boss?

Managing a forest is a big job. How would the kids handle it? They started by electing officers and a president. The leaders would serve for a year. Then there would be a new election.

The officers' main job is deciding how to care for the forest. To do so, the leaders hold meetings with other kids. They also get ideas from teachers, park rangers, and other adults.

In the end, though, the children choose what to do. Then they work together to make it happen. As you can imagine, they've been busy.

Welcome to Our World. *RIGHT: Kids in Peru created this sign. The red shows a trail that they made. The green words say "Children's Forest" in Spanish.*

Kids at Work

Since 2001, the kids have spent a lot of time exploring their land. The Children's Forest is like a never-ending field trip.

For instance, the forest gives kids a chance to be wildlife wizards. By studying footprints and droppings, kids have learned how to track animals. Rain forest creatures include monkeys, sloths, and river otters.

Kids have also made and marked many trails through the Children's Forest. Along the way, they have learned to identify many different kinds of wild plants. In fact, the children used their new knowledge to write a nature guide. It helps visitors to the Children's Forest learn what they are looking at.

The kids have even found ways to make money—without destroying their rain forest. Children collect nuts, seeds, and leaves that fall naturally. Then they use them to make and sell crafts. Money from the sales helps pay for trail signs and other things.

So far, the kids who run the Children's Forest are doing exactly what Joaquín Leguía had hoped. They explore their land. They take care of their land. And they love their land.

 Do you think the Children's Forest is a good idea? What would you do if you had your own forest?

Wild Place. *LEFT: Speeding through the trees, this scarlet macaw is just one of countless rain forest animals. Humans are still learning what lives in rain forests.*

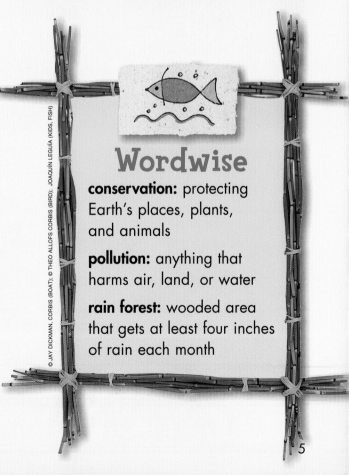

© JAY DICKMAN, CORBIS (BOAT); © THEO ALLOFS CORBIS (BIRD); © JOAQUÍN LEGUÍA (KIDS, FISH)

Wordwise

conservation: protecting Earth's places, plants, and animals

pollution: anything that harms air, land, or water

rain forest: wooded area that gets at least four inches of rain each month

Explore
South America

Peru has many kinds of habitats. There are beaches, deserts, jungles, mountains, and more. These pictures show a little of Peru's variety.

Like Peru, South America has many amazing places. The Andes are the longest mountain range on Earth. The Amazon carries more water than any other river. And huge rain forests grow along the river.

You can learn more about South America by exploring the physical map at right.

Got Trees? *A brown capuchin monkey hangs out in a patch of bamboo. Forests in South America are habitats for many different kinds of monkeys.*

Lost World. *A cactus grows in a dry region near Peru's coast. Behind it lie ruins of an ancient city.*

Winter Coats. *Thick hair keeps alpacas warm.*

North
America

South
America

EQUATOR

SURINAME

FRENCH
GUIANA
(France)

VENEZUELA

GUYANA

COLOMBIA

ECUADOR

Amazon River

Amazon River

P E R U

B R A Z I L

BOLIVIA

PACIFIC
OCEAN

PARAGUAY

ATLANTIC
OCEAN

N

W   E

S

C H I L E

A R G E N T I N A

URUGUAY

Falkland Islands
(United Kingdom)

Map Key

Mountain

Desert

Rain forest

Grassland

Wetland

Rain Forests

Rain forests are amazing places. Did you know that tropical rain forests get up to 400 inches of rain each year? Or that trees in a temperate rain forest can grow hundreds of feet tall? Check out these other rain forest facts.

Tropical Rain Forests

Most rain forests are tropical. They are near the Equator, or the area around the center of Earth. The forests stay warm all year.

Warm air can hold a lot of water. So it rains many times a day. Between storms, the weather is sunny and bright. This mix of sun and rain make the forests very humid.

Plants thrive in these warm, wet forests. In fact, so many plants live here that they fight for light. Tall trees soak up the sunlight high above the forest floor. Smaller plants, such as orchids and vines, grow on the trees to catch more of the sun's rays. The plants are so thick that almost no light reaches the forest floor.

Tropical rain forests provide homes for many kinds of animals. Insects outnumber all other rain forest animals. They crawl across the damp soil and buzz through the humid air. Birds fly through the treetops. Monkeys swing from branch to branch. Large cats creep along limbs looking for food. No matter where you look, you'll find life among the trees.

Tropical rain forests cover less than six percent of Earth's land. Yet they are home to more than half of the planet's plant and animal species. Nowhere else can you find as many kinds of living things all in one place.

At Home in the Heat.
ABOVE: *This gorilla makes its home in a tropical rain forest.* RIGHT: *Along the river, this African rain forest is packed with plants.*

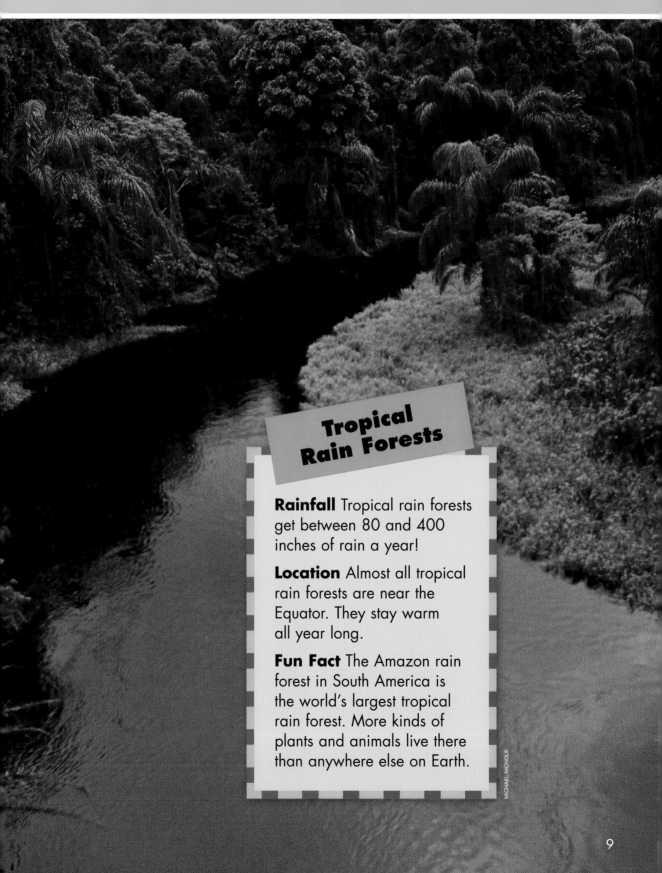

Tropical Rain Forests

Rainfall Tropical rain forests get between 80 and 400 inches of rain a year!

Location Almost all tropical rain forests are near the Equator. They stay warm all year long.

Fun Fact The Amazon rain forest in South America is the world's largest tropical rain forest. More kinds of plants and animals live there than anywhere else on Earth.

MICHAEL NICHOLS

Temperate Rain Forests

Some rain forests are not tropical, but temperate. These forests are farther from the Equator. That means they do not get as hot. Fewer kinds of plants and animals live there too.

One area with temperate rain forests is along the northern Pacific Coast of North America. Summers are warm there, but not hot. Winters are cool, but not cold. Dense fog moves from the ocean to the land. As the air cools, the fog turns into rain. It soaks the forest.

Fewer kinds of plants live in temperate rain forests. Yet many still thrive in this cool, damp environment. Mosses and ferns fill the mist-covered forests. Some trees, such as redwoods, can grow hundreds of feet tall.

Not as many animal species live in temperate rain forests. Those that do are well suited to the cool, wet weather. Squirrels dart through treetops. Marmots, elk, and black-tailed deer nibble on forest plants. Temperate rain forests are home to many kinds of creatures, from beasts to bald eagles.

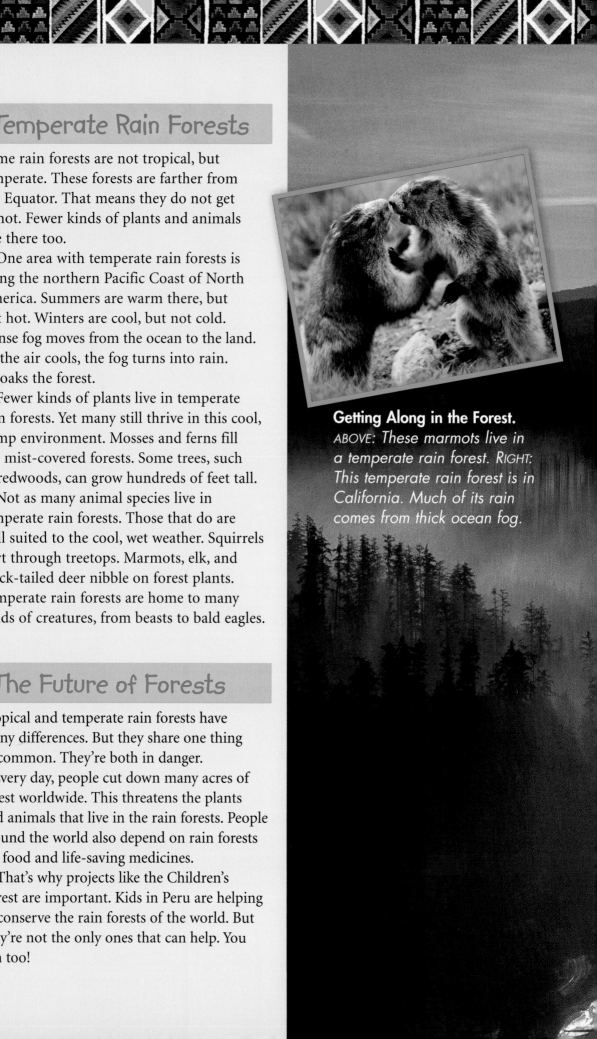

Getting Along in the Forest. ABOVE: *These marmots live in a temperate rain forest.* RIGHT: *This temperate rain forest is in California. Much of its rain comes from thick ocean fog.*

The Future of Forests

Tropical and temperate rain forests have many differences. But they share one thing in common. They're both in danger.

Every day, people cut down many acres of forest worldwide. This threatens the plants and animals that live in the rain forests. People around the world also depend on rain forests for food and life-saving medicines.

That's why projects like the Children's Forest are important. Kids in Peru are helping to conserve the rain forests of the world. But they're not the only ones that can help. You can too!

Temperate Rain Forests

Rainfall Temperate rain forests get about 100 inches of rain a year.

Location Most temperate rain forests are near the western coasts of North America and South America.

Fun Fact The trees in temperate rain forests usually live longer than those in tropical rain forests. Some, such as giant sequoias, can live thousands of years.

SAM ABELL (ANIMALS); JAMES P. BLAIR (FOREST)

Rain Forests

Answer these questions to find out what you've learned about rain forests.

1 What is conservation? Why is conservation sometimes hard?

2 Why are rain forests important?

3 Where is the Children's Forest? What is unusual about it?

4 Where are most rain forests found? Why?

5 How are tropical rain forests like temperate rain forests? How are they different?

JOAQUÍN LEGUÍA